IT'S TIME TO LEARN ABOUT WORLD WAR 1

It's Time to Learn about World War 1

Walter the Educator

Silent King Books
A WhichHead Entertainment Imprint

It's Time to Learn about World War 1 is a collectible little learning book by Walter the Educator that belongs to the Little Learning Books Series. Collect them all and more books at WaltertheEducator.com

WORLD WAR 1

World War I, often referred to as the Great War, was a global conflict that lasted from 1914 to 1918. It was a war that reshaped the geopolitical landscape of the world, resulting in the downfall of empires, significant changes in political boundaries, and the rise of new ideologies. This little book will provide an in-depth look at the origins, major events, consequences, and lasting impacts of World War I, while also highlighting its significance in shaping modern history.

It's Time to Learn about World War 1

Origins of World War I
Nationalism and Imperialism
The late 19th and early 20th centuries were characterized
by rising nationalism and intense imperialism. European
powers were engaged in a race to expand their empires,
particularly in Africa and Asia. The belief in the superiority of
one's nation and the desire to assert dominance over others
contributed to growing tensions among European countries.
Nationalist movements, especially in the Balkans, further
destabilized the region, as ethnic groups sought
independence from the Austro-Hungarian and Ottoman
Empires.

It's Time to Learn about World War 1

Alliance System
By the early 20th century, Europe was divided into two major alliance systems. The Triple Entente, consisting of France, Russia, and the United Kingdom, was formed in response to the perceived threat from the Triple Alliance, which included Germany, Austria-Hungary, and Italy. These alliances were intended to provide mutual defense and deter aggression. However, they also created a situation where a conflict between two countries could quickly escalate into a full-scale war involving multiple nations.

It's Time to Learn about World War 1

Origins of World War I
Nationalism and Imperialism
The late 19th and early 20th centuries were characterized
by rising nationalism and intense imperialism. European
powers were engaged in a race to expand their empires,
particularly in Africa and Asia. The belief in the superiority of
one's nation and the desire to assert dominance over others
contributed to growing tensions among European countries.
Nationalist movements, especially in the Balkans, further
destabilized the region, as ethnic groups sought
independence from the Austro-Hungarian and Ottoman
Empires.

It's Time to Learn about World War 1

Alliance System
By the early 20th century, Europe was divided into two major alliance systems. The Triple Entente, consisting of France, Russia, and the United Kingdom, was formed in response to the perceived threat from the Triple Alliance, which included Germany, Austria-Hungary, and Italy. These alliances were intended to provide mutual defense and deter aggression. However, they also created a situation where a conflict between two countries could quickly escalate into a full-scale war involving multiple nations.

It's Time to Learn about World War 1

Militarism and the Arms Race
The period leading up to World War I saw a significant
buildup of military forces and weapons. European powers
believed that maintaining strong armies and navies was
essential to protect their interests and maintain their status
as global powers.

It's Time to Learn
about World War 1

This arms race, particularly between Germany and Britain, created an atmosphere of suspicion and competition. The widespread belief in the inevitability of war also contributed to military planning that emphasized rapid mobilization and offensive strategies.

It's Time to Learn about World War 1

The Assassination of Archduke Franz Ferdinand
The immediate spark that ignited World War I was the assassination of Archduke Franz Ferdinand of Austria-Hungary on June 28, 1914, in Sarajevo, Bosnia. Ferdinand and his wife, Sophie, were killed by Gavrilo Princip, a member of a Serbian nationalist group known as the Black Hand. The assassination was a protest against Austro-Hungarian rule in the Balkans, and it set off a chain of events that quickly spiraled out of control.

It's Time to Learn about World War 1

Austria-Hungary, with the backing of Germany, issued an ultimatum to Serbia, demanding a series of harsh concessions.

It's Time to Learn about World War 1

When Serbia refused to fully comply, Austria-Hungary declared war on Serbia on July 28, 1914. This triggered a series of mobilizations and declarations of war, as alliances were activated, and soon, much of Europe was engulfed in conflict.

It's Time to Learn about World War 1

The Course of the War
The Western Front
The war on the Western Front, primarily fought between Germany and the Allies (France, Britain, and later the United States), is perhaps the most famous aspect of World War I. The early months of the war were marked by rapid movement, as German forces advanced through Belgium into France, hoping to quickly defeat the French in accordance with the Schlieffen Plan. However, the German advance was halted at the First Battle of the Marne in September 1914, and the war on the Western Front soon devolved into a stalemate.

It's Time to Learn about World War 1

When Serbia refused to fully comply, Austria-Hungary declared war on Serbia on July 28, 1914. This triggered a series of mobilizations and declarations of war, as alliances were activated, and soon, much of Europe was engulfed in conflict.

It's Time to Learn about World War 1

The Course of the War
The Western Front
The war on the Western Front, primarily fought between Germany and the Allies (France, Britain, and later the United States), is perhaps the most famous aspect of World War I. The early months of the war were marked by rapid movement, as German forces advanced through Belgium into France, hoping to quickly defeat the French in accordance with the Schlieffen Plan. However, the German advance was halted at the First Battle of the Marne in September 1914, and the war on the Western Front soon devolved into a stalemate.

It's Time to Learn about World War 1

Trench warfare became the defining feature of the Western Front. Both sides dug elaborate networks of trenches, stretching from the Belgian coast to the Swiss border. Soldiers lived in horrific conditions, facing constant danger from artillery bombardments, machine-gun fire, and poison gas attacks. Major battles, such as the Battle of Verdun (1916) and the Battle of the Somme (1916) resulted in massive casualties but little territorial gain.

It's Time to Learn about World War 1

The Eastern Front
The war on the Eastern Front was more fluid, with larger movements of troops and fewer entrenched positions. The Russian Empire faced off against the Central Powers, primarily Germany and Austria-Hungary.

It's Time to Learn about World War 1

Early Russian successes were followed by devastating defeats, particularly at the Battle of Tannenberg in August 1914. The Russian war effort was hampered by internal political instability, logistical challenges, and a lack of industrial capacity.

It's Time to Learn about World War 1

By 1917, the Russian people were suffering from severe food shortages and war fatigue, leading to the Russian Revolution and the eventual withdrawal of Russia from the war.

It's Time to Learn about World War 1

Other Fronts and Global Involvement
World War I was truly a global conflict, with fighting taking place not only in Europe but also in the Middle East, Africa, and Asia. In the Middle East, the British supported Arab revolts against the Ottoman Empire, leading to the eventual disintegration of Ottoman control over much of the region. In Africa, European colonies became battlegrounds as forces from Germany and the Allies clashed. Japan, allied with Britain, took control of German colonies in the Pacific and China.

It's Time to Learn about World War 1

The war also had a significant impact on the home fronts of the belligerent nations. Governments implemented rationing, censorship, and propaganda campaigns to maintain public support for the war effort.

It's Time to Learn about World War 1

Other Fronts and Global Involvement
World War I was truly a global conflict, with fighting taking place not only in Europe but also in the Middle East, Africa, and Asia. In the Middle East, the British supported Arab revolts against the Ottoman Empire, leading to the eventual disintegration of Ottoman control over much of the region. In Africa, European colonies became battlegrounds as forces from Germany and the Allies clashed. Japan, allied with Britain, took control of German colonies in the Pacific and China.

It's Time to Learn about World War 1

The war also had a significant impact on the home fronts of the belligerent nations. Governments implemented rationing, censorship, and propaganda campaigns to maintain public support for the war effort.

It's Time to Learn about World War 1

Women played an increasingly important role in the workforce, taking on jobs traditionally held by men who were now serving in the military.

It's Time to Learn about World War 1

The Entry of the United States
The United States initially sought to remain neutral in the conflict, but a combination of factors eventually led to its entry into the war in 1917.

It's Time to Learn about World War 1

One of the key factors was the resumption of unrestricted submarine warfare by Germany, which led to the sinking of several American ships.

It's Time to Learn about World War 1

Additionally, the interception of the Zimmermann Telegram, in which Germany proposed an alliance with Mexico against the United States, further inflamed American public opinion.

It's Time to Learn about World War 1

The entry of the United States into the war provided a significant boost to the Allies, both in terms of manpower and industrial capacity. American troops, known as the American Expeditionary Forces (AEF), played a crucial role in the final offensives on the Western Front, helping to tip the balance in favor of the Allies.

It's Time to Learn about World War 1

The End of the War and the Treaty of Versailles
The Armistice

It's Time to Learn about World War 1

The entry of the United States into the war provided a significant boost to the Allies, both in terms of manpower and industrial capacity. American troops, known as the American Expeditionary Forces (AEF), played a crucial role in the final offensives on the Western Front, helping to tip the balance in favor of the Allies.

It's Time to Learn about World War 1

The End of the War and the Treaty of Versailles
The Armistice

It's Time to Learn about World War 1

By 1918, the Central Powers were on the brink of collapse. Germany, in particular, was facing severe food shortages, economic strain, and widespread discontent among its population.

It's Time to Learn about World War 1

The failure of the German spring offensives in 1918, combined with the growing strength of the Allied forces, forced Germany to seek an armistice. On November 11, 1918, an armistice was signed, effectively ending the fighting on the Western Front. The war was over, but the process of negotiating peace was just beginning.

It's Time to Learn about World War 1

The Treaty of Versailles
The Treaty of Versailles, signed on June 28, 1919, was the most significant of the peace treaties that officially ended World War I. The treaty imposed harsh penalties on Germany, including the loss of territory, the reduction of its military, and the payment of reparations. Perhaps the most controversial aspect of the treaty was the "war guilt clause," which placed sole responsibility for the war on Germany and its allies.

It's Time to Learn about World War 1

The Treaty of Versailles had far-reaching consequences. Many Germans viewed the treaty as a humiliation and a betrayal, sowing the seeds of resentment that would later contribute to the rise of Adolf Hitler and the outbreak of World War II.

It's Time to Learn about World War 1

Additionally, the redrawing of national boundaries in Europe and the Middle East created new states but also left many ethnic groups dissatisfied, leading to ongoing tensions in the years that followed.

It's Time to Learn about World War 1

The Impact and Legacy of World War I
Political and Social Changes
World War I had profound political and social
consequences. The war led to the collapse of four major
empires: the German Empire, the Austro-Hungarian Empire,
the Ottoman Empire, and the Russian Empire.

It's Time to Learn about World War 1

Additionally, the redrawing of national boundaries in Europe and the Middle East created new states but also left many ethnic groups dissatisfied, leading to ongoing tensions in the years that followed.

It's Time to Learn about World War 1

The Impact and Legacy of World War I
Political and Social Changes
World War I had profound political and social consequences. The war led to the collapse of four major empires: the German Empire, the Austro-Hungarian Empire, the Ottoman Empire, and the Russian Empire.

It's Time to Learn about World War 1

In their place, new nations were created, including Czechoslovakia, Yugoslavia, and Poland. In Russia, the Bolshevik Revolution of 1917 resulted in the establishment of the first communist state, which would have a significant impact on global politics for the remainder of the 20th century.

It's Time to Learn about World War 1

The war also had a lasting impact on social structures and gender roles. The large-scale mobilization of men for the war effort meant that women were required to take on new roles in the workforce.

It's Time to Learn about World War 1

While many women were forced to return to traditional roles after the war, the experience contributed to the growing momentum for women's suffrage, with women gaining the right to vote in several countries in the years following the war.

It's Time to Learn about World War 1

Technological and Military Innovations
World War I saw the introduction of new military
technologies that would change the nature of warfare
forever.

It's Time to Learn about World War 1

The use of tanks, airplanes, and submarines marked the beginning of modern mechanized warfare. Chemical weapons, such as mustard gas and chlorine gas, were used for the first time, leading to horrific injuries and long-lasting health effects for those exposed.

It's Time to Learn about World War 1

The war also highlighted the importance of logistics, mass production, and the coordination of military resources on a large scale. These lessons would be applied in future conflicts, particularly during World War II.

It's Time to Learn about World War 1

The reparations imposed on Germany by the Treaty of Versailles further exacerbated economic problems, contributing to the hyperinflation that plagued the country in the early 1920s.

It's Time to Learn about World War 1

Economic Consequences
The economic consequences of World War I were severe,
particularly for Europe. The war caused widespread
destruction of infrastructure, industries, and agricultural land,
leading to economic instability and inflation.

It's Time to Learn
about World War 1

The global economy also experienced significant shifts as a result of the war. The United States emerged as a dominant economic power, while European countries faced mounting debts and economic challenges. The post-war economic instability would contribute to the onset of the Great Depression in the 1930s.

It's Time to Learn about World War 1

Cultural Impact

World War I had a profound cultural impact, particularly on literature, art, and philosophy. The brutality and senselessness of the war led many intellectuals and artists to question traditional values and beliefs. The disillusionment experienced by many veterans and civilians found expression in the works of writers such as Erich Maria Remarque, whose novel *All Quiet on the Western Front* depicted the horrors of trench warfare.

It's Time to Learn about World War 1

The war also gave rise to new artistic movements, such as Dadaism, which rejected the logic and reason that had seemingly led to the destruction of an entire generation. The "Lost Generation" of writers and artists, including figures like Ernest Hemingway and F. Scott Fitzgerald, reflected the profound sense of alienation and despair that followed the war.

It's Time to Learn about World War 1

Conclusion

World War I was a cataclysmic event that reshaped the world in ways that are still felt today. It marked the end of an era of European dominance and the beginning of a new geopolitical order. The war's causes, from nationalism and imperialism to the alliance system and militarism, underscore the complexity of the factors that led to such a devastating conflict. Its impact, both immediate and long-lasting, can be seen in the political, social, economic, and cultural changes that followed.

The legacy of World War I serves as a reminder of the dangers of unchecked nationalism, militarism, and political alliances. It also highlights the importance of diplomacy, international cooperation, and efforts to prevent the kinds of conflicts that led to one of the deadliest wars in human history.

ABOUT THE CREATOR

Walter the Educator is one of the
pseudonyms for Walter Anderson.
Formally educated in Chemistry,
Business, and Education, he is an
educator, an author, a diverse
entrepreneur, and he is the son
of a disabled war veteran.
"Walter the Educator" shares his
time between educating and creating.
He holds interests and owns several
creative projects that entertain,
enlighten, enhance, and educate,
hoping to inspire and motivate you.
Follow, find new works, and stay
up to date with Walter the Educator™

at WaltertheEducator.com

Milton Keynes UK
Ingram Content Group UK Ltd.
UKHW020109181024
449757UK00012B/756